Activate Your Vision Board

Learn How to Set Goals, Take Action
&
Get Your Vision off the Board
And
Into Your Life in 40 Days or Less

Lucinda Cross

Bronx, New York

www.lucindacross.com

Editing-Formatting: Robin Devonish, The Self-Publishing Maven

Interior Layout Design: Joy E. Turner, JetSet Communications & Consulting

Limits of Liability ~ Disclaimer

The purpose of this book is to educate and share. The author and publisher do not guarantee that anyone following these techniques, suggestions, tips, ideas, or strategies will become successful. The author and publisher shall have neither liability nor responsibility to anyone with respect to any loss of, damage caused or alleged to be caused, directly or indirectly by the information contained in this book.

ISBN 13: 978-0-9905629-1-7

ISBN 10: 0990562913

Printed in the United States of America

Contents

Foreword

And the Lord answered me, and said, Write the vision, and make it plain upon tables, that he may run that readeth it. - Habakkuk 2:2, The Holy Bible (KJV)

There will always be an excuse to hide, play small, speak low, settle for less, procrastinate and pretend that your desires are "too much, too big and too complex".

There will always be a reason to believe that you are incompetent, incapable, unworthy and undeserving of the mission, vision and life purpose that God has placed in your hands.

Deep in your heart you know that God wants you to embrace and embody perfect health, lavish wealth, loving, harmonious relationships and the freedom of creative self-expression.

Deep in your heart you know that you came here to love and be loved, heal and be healed.

Deep in your heart you know that you've been meddling in mediocrity and stepping over dollars to pick up dimes.

Deep in your heart you know that authenticity has no competition. You know that what God has for you, is for YOU.

So STOP.

Stop looking outside of yourself for affirmation, confirmation, and validation.

Look within your own heart and define abundance, prosperity, wealth and success on your terms.

Lucinda Cross IS a sacred and divine daughter of God filled with love, purpose, passion and unlimited potential.

In Activate Your Vision, she invites you to acknowledge what you desire and clarify exactly what it all means to YOU.

Let today be the day that you walk towards the desires of your heart.

Kadena Tate

Business Acceleration Alchemist

A Warm Introduction

Welcome to an amazing journey of creating your vision board. This book is a playbook that will guide you through questions and activities as you dream, cultivate, and manifest your best year yet.

There will be both spiritual and practical awakenings. The three things I love to do are Dream big, Create the vision, and Make those dreams become a reality. When you think about the terms Activate, Vision, and Goals, you automatically seek to define your purpose and how to obtain it. Your purpose is the legacy that you will always be remembered for, rewarded for, and acknowledged. Living life without a plan is like driving in an unknown area without a map. It is a journey of being lost. That is why I decided to pen this playbook; to help you activate your vision by acknowledging your purpose and passion, setting and accomplishing goals, and remaining committed to the journey.

Remember, YOU are Amazing and YOU are about to show the world!

Lucinda Cross

Chief Activator and Your Go-To-Girl to Get Stuff Done

Playbook Rules

Activating Rule #1:
It can be HARD, or you can make it EASY

Activating Rule #2:
Go deeper in your thoughts and answers

Activating Rule #3:
Give yourself permission

Give yourself permission to succeed. After you acknowledge your God Given Right, start your journey by filling out this playbook as best you can.

Use the Activate Your Vision planner to keep your notes or make a folder specifically for your vision.

There is an online version of the journal you can download at www.lucindacross.com. Or you can purchase a hard copy at www.amazon.com Throughout this playbook, there are affirmations you can cut out and pin up on your board.

Use Pinterest or the Activate Your Vision app to take pictures and write your goals along this journey.

Important Notice: There is no right or wrong way to create a vision. There are no obligations or prerequisites for turning your vision into a reality. Do whatever makes you feel happy, loving, healthy, and peaceful. If a task feels too complicated, drop it. This playbook is designed to help you live a life of fire, fun, and freedom.

Put the Current Year

Everything is
complete, nothing is
broke, and nothing
is missing

I am full of purpose to lead the

life I desire, the power to bring

my dreams to fruition, and

passion never to give up.

For the first part of your journey through this playbook, I want you to reflect on your previous year. Reflection leads to clarity. To set goals, create your vision, and take action, you must be clear about your hopes, dreams, and aspirations. To gain this clarity and move on your journey, I want you to answer the following questions:

Put the previous year

I learned:

1._____

2._____

3._____

This was the year I experienced:

1._____

2._____

3._____

This was the year I started:

1._____

2._____

3._____

This was the year I stopped:

1._____

2._____

3._____

I was proud of myself for:

1._____

2._____

3._____

I release the following feelings:

1._____

2._____

3._____

What dreams came true?

1._____

2._____

3._____

Personal transformation took place because of the following:

1._____

2._____

3._____

I let go of the following:

1._____

2._____

3._____

As a result of letting go I was able to:

1._____

2._____

3._____

The most amazing thing I discovered about myself was:

1._____

2._____

3._____

Last year led me to do:

1._____

2._____

3._____

Last year led me to be:

1._____

2._____

3._____

I am grateful for the following:

1._____

2._____

3._____

Self-Examination

Who Do You Think You Are?

1._____

2._____

3._____

Who Did You Think You Were Before?

1._____

2._____

3._____

Who Do You Think You Are Becoming?

1._____

2._____

3._____

What held you back in the past?

_____

_____

_____

What is the lie you keep telling yourself?

_____

_____

_____

What are you resisting?

_____

_____

_____

Where do you limit self?

_____

_____

_____

What am are you unwilling to risk?

_____

_____

_____

Where do you hold back?

_____

_____

_____

What are you withholding?

_____

_____

_____

Where are you too comfortable?

_____

_____

_____

What agitates you? Agitation is a short cut to action.

_____

_____

_____

Helpful Hints Along Your Journey

Create a Gratitude Jar.

Get an empty jar or visit your local dollar store and purchase a mason jar. Feel free to decorate it, or you can purchase a premade Gratitude Jar from the Activate Pop- Up Shop. We have some cool, signature handcrafted jars. Visit www.activateyourvisionkit.com.

Every day you put in a little note of what you are grateful for in your life. I like to do mine right before I go to bed. I get a small piece of paper and write down one thing I was grateful for, for that day.

Maybe it was finding a parking spot when I was running late for a meeting. Maybe it was the fact that my teenager threw out the trash in the morning. Maybe it is the fact that I received that favorable response I have been waiting for all year long.

In your Gratitude Jar write the following:

I breathe life and give thanks for all that has passed.

I open my heart to the amazing opportunities that are happening before me.

I release all that is and no longer serving me.

I accept and activate light and peace in my life, and all is well.

Now that you have clarity from your previous year, you can begin focusing on your current year and what you want to manifest into reality. Do this by answering the following questions:

ACTIVATING YOUR VISION FOR

_____

Put the current year

What do you most desire to experience?

1.

2.

3.

Make some bold declarations:

1.

2.

3.

This year I give myself permission to do the following:

1.

2.

3.

This year will be the year that I:

1.

2.

3.

This year I will commit to doing the following:

1.

2.

3.

The next step in your journey is to list 99 things you promise to do this year. 99 things may seem like a lot, but remember there are 365 days this year. This perspective will help you realize you have time to accomplish 99 hopes, dreams, and aspirations. Make this list fun and joyful. Writing this list should be a freeing experience. Be creative and let your limitlessness shine through!

99 Things I Promise To Do In

_____

Put the Current Year

1. _____

2. _____

3. _____

4. _____

5. _____

6. _____

7. _____

8. _____

9. _____

10._____

11._____

12._____

13._____

14._____

15._____

16._____

17._____

18._____

19._____

20._____

21._____

22._____

23._____

24._____

25._____

26._____

27._____

28._____

29._____

30._____

31._____

32._____

33._____

34._____

35._____

36._____

37._____

38._____

39._____

40._____

41._____

42._____

43._____

44._____

45._____

46._____

47._____

48._____

49._____

50._____

51._____

52._____

53._____

54._____

55._____

56._____

57._____

58._____

59._____

60._____

61._____

62._____

63._____

64._____

65._____

66._____

67._____

68._____

69._____

70._____

71._____

72._____

73._____

74._____

75._____

76._____

77._____

78._____

79._____

80._____

81._____

82._____

83._____

84._____

85._____

86._____

87._____

88._____

89._____

90._____

91._____

92._____

93._____

94._____

95._____

96._____

97._____

98._____

99._____

Helpful Hints Along Your Journey

Things to do when you don't feel activated, and your motivation is very underwhelmed.

Life is not always gumdrops and bubble gum. You will not always wake up feeling like a superhero. There will be those days, yes those days when you want to throw in the towel. First, cut a piece of towel out and paste it on this page. The piece of the towel will remind you that you cannot give up. You must look at this cloth and laugh, pray, and keep moving forward. Next, create a list of things you'll do to reinvigorate your spirit so that you can continue your journey to success. Then, when you're feeling defeated, look at the list you created. These are things you'll do IN CASE OF EMERGENCY to pick yourself up again.

Here are some examples of things I do when I'm feeling defeated:

- Take a power nap

- Take a bubble bath

- Polish my nails

- Eat my favorite cheat meal

- Put on my favorite song from when I was younger

- Go outside and let out a big yell

- Cry

As I think about my years that passed, I think about the lessons of humility and vulnerability life was teaching me. Humility and vulnerability are the hardest lessons life has taught me thus far. I also learned to be fully present in the moment. I often would be in attendance but not present in life's rewards and warning signs. I learned how to stay grounded in prayer and the importance of being active with my children versus spending money, spending time.

Here are a few lessons life will teach you along your journey:

- Don't let your obstacles and challenges discourage you from reaching your goals.

- It is never too late to start toward your goals.

- Goals are guides that need to be reviewed on a frequent basis and altered as needed.

- You don't achieve your goals by yourself. Other people, whom I call your guardian angels, help you along the way. You must remember to acknowledge those who've helped you on your path toward success.

- Sometimes you need someone to do to you what birds do to their young: kick them out of the nest.

I would like for you to Love yourself right where you are…with what you have and don't have.

You are gifted and loved. You are strong and courageous. You are an incredible point of light.

Get Rid of the Routine and Create Rituals

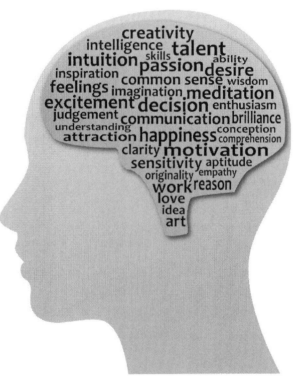

I have often heard empowerment coaches or therapist ask their clients, "What are your goals in life?" or "What are your short/long-term goals?" But very few have ever truly defined the word goal. We all live complex lives that require us to figure out our goals, understand our purpose, and how goals could hinder or create a movement in our underlining mission. But, when you clearly understand the purpose behind the goal and how it aligns within your life, then and only then, will things start to activate.

According to Merriam-Webster Dictionary, the term "Goal."

"Goal" means: something that you are trying to do or achieve.

Now let's look at Achieve:

"Achieve" means: to get or reach (something) by working hard; to get or attain as the result of exertion; to become successful.

I highlighted the two terms **Goal** and **Achieve** because with every goal you set, you must maintain faith to achieve it. What's the purpose of setting goals that you know you can't or won't achieve? Right!! Nothing is impossible when it comes to setting goals, but you should set goals that you're passionate, committed, and are dedicated. I often hear people say, "The devil will intercept your vision with failure, trials, and rejection just to make you give up." However, the first thing you must understand about goals and executing them is that you'll fail at them before you succeed with them. That's life and the way the cookie crumbles, but you should never allow those situations to hinder your goal of succeeding. According to Forbes Magazine (Feinstein, Ashley, 2014) "Why you should be writing down your goals." There are four steps for creating clear and measurable goals that will lead you to huge success.

1. **Create a Vision** ~ The first step to creating a goal is to figure out what you want. If you don't know what you want, you don't know what you need to achieve to get there.

2. **Make it Measurable** ~ Take your vision and turn it into a written list of concrete

goals. Choose an achievable timeframe to accomplish your goals, as well as measurable details, so you know exactly when you've achieved them.

3. **Set Benchmarks** ~ Benchmarks are a great way to keep you on track. These are the milestones you set for the completion of your goals. You may find you're moving more quickly or slowly than you expected. That's not a problem; you can adjust! Adjust your expectations and timeline as you gather more information while achieving your benchmarks.

4. **Celebrate your Success** ~ The most important part of goal-setting is celebrating your successes. How will you reward yourself for hitting your benchmarks along the way? How will you celebrate once you've reached your goal? Celebrating your achievements helps you maintain the efforts and creates enjoyment as you journey through to your destination.

Every year people make New Year's Resolutions. Unfortunately, they drive you crazy by midyear. When you think about the goals you've previously set and things you wanted to achieve in life, I want you to think about what hindered you and what motivated you. Were you confident and believed in yourself enough to know that your goals could one day come true? I want you to scratch the resolutions and create a ritual to dream BIG.

Continuing your journey, I want you to answer the following questions with enormous intention. These are your BIG goals.

My big financial goal for this year is:

_____

_____

_____

My big fitness goal for this year is:

_____

_____

_____

My big business or career goal this year is:

_____

_____

_____

My big spiritual goal for this year is:

_____

_____

_____

My big family and friendship goals this year are:

_____

_____

_____

My big personal goal for this year is:

_____

_____

_____

My big and bold goal that seems impossible is:

_____

_____

_____

Time for Some Action!!!

Now that you've listed your BIG goals for this year, the next step is to document them. Write the vision and make it plain. Use your Activate Your

Vision Journal, and on a separate page, write down each of your goals. Under each of your goals, write down the steps you need to take for each goal. For example,

Goal: Finish My Book

Steps:

- Write my outline (next week)

- Create writing schedule (1 hour every Monday-Wednesday-Friday at 6 am)

- Create a publishing budget (save 15% of every paycheck)

- Research self-publishers

- Research book cover designers

- Create an Author Vision Board

It's important to include actionable steps and things you can begin doing now versus later. Adding a time frame next to your actionable steps makes it easier to complete. If your steps seem too vague, break them down into mini-steps. Accomplishing goals shouldn't feel like a punishment. Instead, it should feel like a reward for getting closer to becoming a published author.

Please remember, you don't have to write down every step needed to accomplish your goal, just jot down the ones you can work on immediately. Once you complete each step, you can move forward. Create actionable goals.

Create Rituals that are worth Celebrating

Rituals give you the freedom to get rid of your to-do list, and focus on doing the things that matter the most to you. I like to create my calendar and weekly agenda using unique titles and themes. March is always Magnificent March. April is Communication Month. I break my weeks into reminders. Marketing Mondays, Domestic Tuesdays, Writing Wednesdays, Date Night Thursdays (with my Hubby or the kids),

Faithful Fridays, etc.

Now let's create some motivating titles can you give your months. List them below.

_____

_____

_____

_____

_____

_____

_____

_____

_____

_____

_____

What can you name your days of the week? Remember, you can change them from month to month depending on your focus and your priorities.

_____

_____

_____

_____

_____

_____

_____

Love is in the Air

Another step, which I believe is crucial to your success, is to write yourself a love letter. I want you to write this letter using positive words and filled with messages of support. It must include all the things you need to hear throughout the year to feel love and support from yourself. The object of this exercise is to empower yourself. You can start the letter any way you like and end it any way you like. The only thing you cannot do is write anything disempowering or from a place of fear. Deal? Deal. Start writing.

Below are some starter sentences you can include. Of course, feel free to make up your own.

Dear radiant and wonderful me,

This year I would like to learn how to:

_____

_____

_____

This is the year I will give myself the gift of:

_____

_____

_____

This year I will release more:

_____

_____

_____

This year I would like to celebrate my birthday, anniversary, etc. by:

_____

_____

_____

I love you!

Signed,

Dated:

Helpful Hints Along Your Journey

Eat a Bowl of Habits for Breakfast

Start your morning off with a healthy habit meal.

1. Focus your attention on a single task for the day.
2. Avoid checking your inbox first thing in the morning.
3. Take 5 to 10 minutes to meditate.

The key to executing any goal in life is to exude high levels of confidence, belief, and faith in yourself. The way you feel about yourself as a person, the way you acknowledge your potential, and the way you desire more for yourself, dictates just how successful you'll become at achieving your goals.

Researchers say it takes about 21 days to learn a new habit. Eating this healthy habit meal will take your life to the next level by aligning your mind, body, and spirit.

Affirmations

Feel free to cut these affirmations out and add them to your Vision Board

I now dissolve the habit of putting off difficult tasks

All blocks to setting and achieving my goals have dissolved now.

On the soul level, I release all fear of failure.

Understanding Goals

Activating Your Vision requires you to have a clear understanding of your goals and the task required to complete those goals.

Goals, as I stated before, are things you want to achieve. But before you can achieve a goal, you must first know what it is you want to do and within what timeframe. Knowing your time frame for achieving your goals is essential to the overall achievement and success of what it is you have planned. To make this easy, professionals have categorized goal-setting into two elements, "Short-Term" or "Long-Term". Categorizing your goals prevents confusion and gives you timeframe order. This way you can plan and execute your goals with ease while still living the life you deem necessary. Before you can plan or categorize any goal, you must be able to answer the following questions:

- **What do I want to accomplish?**

- **What changes or enhancers do I want to see?**

- **How long do I want this process to take?**

- **How much money will it require?**

- **Can I achieve this alone, or do I need to invest in a team?**

- **Is this goal necessary in the overall scheme of my life's purpose?**

Once you can answer each question for each goal, you're ready to prioritize them and make them fit into your daily life. Organizing your goals will help keep everything in perspective and in real-time for you. This way you don't get discouraged, frustrated, upset, or frazzled when life unexpectedly throws you a curveball.

Now that you have a clear vision of what you want to achieve, it's time to determine if your goals are "short-term" or "long-term". Deciding this will help maintain focus, progress, and you're already busy business schedule. "Short-term goals" are defined as priorities that can are accomplished anywhere from within one day up to two years. Some examples of this time frame are; stay away from negativity, set up a checking and savings account, and cut out unnecessary spending. These activities are things we can do within an hour or a plan that can grow over time with consistency and determination. On the other hand, "Long-term goals" are goals that take more than a year to accomplish and may require regular savings. The best examples of this type of timeframe are saying that you plan to be a multi-millionaire by the age of 50. Or, trying to obtain your masters or doctorate, writing and publishing a novel, and purchasing a home. Long-term goals require time and money because they're normally the elevation to your already purposeful life. When people plan long-term goals, they seek greater results and happiness that will help them enjoy life more abundantly. However, some people plan their long-term goals within what they call a 5, 10, and 15-year plans. This action gives them successes in working forward to. Also, some people take the requirements of their long-term goals and break them down, so they can manage them. Then complete them within five years, instead of trying to achieve one big thing at once. The way you choose to execute your goals is solely up to you, but making sure they're manageable, achievable, and rewarding is what's most important.

Affirmations

I visualize the achievement of my goal
daily.

I recognize the barriers to achieving
my goals, and I move around them,
over them and through them.

I let go of a life without goals and
replace it with a destiny of success
and grand achievement.

On Your Mark. Get Set. Go!

Goal-Setting

Now that you've defined your goals and prioritized them let's look at the importance of setting them. Some will say that goal-setting is as simple as saying what you want to accomplish. Others will suggest that you should think about what you want to do and write it down. Very few will say that goals don't exist because everything that can happen in your life is already ordained to happen. But the key to achieving any goal is to activate them. Goals must be nurtured, worked, prayed for, and fought to keep. They require your movement. Goals will not just happen, they're not miracles that come alive with the touch of a wand. They are activities in life that you have to work hard to achieve. Some goals will require you to sacrifice your well-being, compromise your finances, re-elevate your friends and family, and risk your lifestyle so that you can say "mission accomplished." But when setting goals, you need to investigate fully and clearly think about the risks and challenges you'll face.

For example, with the unstableness of our job market, creating multiple income streams is extremely necessary for people to live comfortably. Living on one source of income has become such a daunting task that many people can't fathom it anymore. Therefore, the hustle to become an entrepreneur and start a business has heightened. However, people are creating other streams of income without doing the learning, networking, or getting a full understanding of the business they are seeking to engage. **First mistake!!!** Whenever you plan a goal of gaining more money, you must know the industry and understand how to achieve within it so that your efforts can be prosperous. How do you expect to build a multimillion dollar business if you don't know the business itself? This action is all a part of goal-setting; educating yourself on your goals and creating realistic deadlines. And, is essential to the success of your journey! In all my years of being an entrepreneur, the most important thing I ask people when they approached me about supporting their business is:

- **What is your underlying message and purpose?**

- **What is it that you ultimately wanted to achieve?**

- **How much will it cost you to get there?**

These three questions are what potential partners, investors, and companies want specific and clear answers to.

I have yet to find a financial investor who's willing to give money to a person who's not clear on their business plan or hasn't tested their objective. Not to mention someone who doesn't have a comprehensive budget. I want you to look strategically at your goals, and what you need to achieve them effectively. You can use this same concept when trying to plan and execute personal goals. Understanding your goal will help you save time, money, and energy. Ultimately, it'll help you obtain the support. In addition to all of that, knowing the complexities of your goals will give you the primary information necessary to set them properly. Setting goals is more than just saying, "I want to become a doctor" or "In five years I see myself out of debt, married and preparing for retirement." Those are merely statements that you wish to achieve. But setting them and activating is something that requires thought, planning, and self-realization. Here are my seven rules for goal-setting to help you carefully set rewarding goals that are meaningful.

- **Set Goals that Motivate You**
- **Be Free and Don't Be Attached To The Outcome**
- **Put It In Writing**
- **Create A Course Of Action**
- **Remain Committed**
- **Heart-centered goal-setting**
- **Activate Don't Procrastinate**

From this list, I want to elaborate on the concept of heart-centered goal-setting. The simple fact is that for goals to be powerful, they should come from your heart. When you set goals from your heart, they'll manifest. When you set goals from anywhere else, they just cause you to feel overwhelmed and cause you to be stressed out. Your goals can have structure, can be trackable, and can have a timeframe of attainability, but if they're not heart-centered, you're doomed to fail.

Almost everyone sets goals, chooses power words, and creates to-do lists as long as the Nile River of what they want to accomplish this year. The problem with this is we let these other people's desires creep into our minds and sow seeds of fear. Your inner critic will plant the idea in your head that your goals aren't big enough or bold enough and will cause your ambition wilt away before you even start trying to achieve your goals.

To defeat this, you must set heart-centered goals. Be free from the limitations your inner critic places on you. Just be in the present. This magical moment, here and now, is all you truly have. Silence your inner critic and have fun goal-setting!

The trick to overcoming the mindset that your goals aren't good enough is not to worry about what everyone else is doing. When your goals come from your heart, they become your Truth and not everyone else's.

Take this moment to wipe your slate clean, to remove any negative emotion attached to your goals not being good enough, and to give yourself a fresh start. This moment is freeing, and you're worthy.

A lot of you might be wondering how to tell if your goals are your Truth. Start by asking yourself, "Does this goal make my body swell with anticipation?" If it does, you'll feel your shoulders pull back from pride, your lips form a smile, and your heart open. If it doesn't, you'll feel your shoulders slouch from dread, your lips form a grimace, and your heart close. If your body doesn't expand with excitement, your goal isn't your Truth. It's someone else's.

For example, let's say your intention is to stop eating sugar. Imagine six weeks have passed. You remain steadfast, but suddenly you experience a craving and fall off the wagon. Then, you start beating yourself up for failing.

STOP! Ask yourself, "Do I truly want to quit eating sugar or am I doing this because everyone else is?" If your goal isn't your own, you'll never achieve it. It's not your Truth.

To set a heart-centered goal; you must make sure they're coming from the right place. If they're heart-centered, they'll pump passion through your veins. They'll be your 'Truth' and something that you truly desire.

Remember, you shouldn't suffer in 'Fear Town' from your goals. You're meant to play, to love, to be your unique self, and to be of service during your goal-setting experience. So please pay attention and notice when you're in Fear Town. Leave that polluted, one-horse place. Head to Fun City instead. This place is where your goals will invigorate your soul.

For the next part of your goal-setting plan, I would like you to research your goals and learn the history, the trend, the success, the requirements, and the percentage of successful achievers. Knowing all of this will allow you the opportunity to plan, prepare, and pursue the right opportunities, which will take you to the right people who can help make your goals come true. There is nothing like going to a car dealership and saying, "I want to purchase a car," but not knowing the kind of car you want and why. Is it low maintenance? Is it great with gas mileage? This minor example is the same with everything you obtain or achieve throughout life. So I would like for you to create two goals and answer the questions below.

Goal #1
(Write it here)

_____

_____

_____

What do you know about the goal?

_____

_____

_____

Is it a Long or Short-Term Goal?

_____

_____

_____

What is the purpose of the goal?

_____

_____

_____

What are the benefits of achieving it?

_____

_____

_____

What are the risks associated with achieving it?

_____

_____

_____

When do you see yourself finalizing the work on your dream?

_____

_____

_____

Are you committed to maintaining the goal?

_____

_____

_____

Goal #2
(Write it here)

_____

_____

_____

What do you know about the goal?

_____

_____

_____

Is it a Long or Short-Term Goal?

_____

_____

_____

What is the purpose of the goal?

_____

_____

_____

What are the benefits of achieving it?

_____

_____

_____

What are the risks associated with achieving it?

_____

_____

_____

When do you see yourself finalizing the work on your dream?

_____

_____

_____

Are you committed to maintaining the goal?

_____

_____

_____

As you noticed, I threw the concept of commitment in there. I did this because there's nothing like setting up a bunch of goals, knowing that you can't commit to them. Sometimes achieving goals can take a lot of blood, sweat, tears, and years before you finally make it across the finish line. Everyone can't handle or prepare for a challenge like this, so before you take on any goal, I want you to soul-search. Decide within the depths of your heart, "Am I ready to commit to this?", "Do I have what it takes?", and no matter what "I won't give up, and I am willing to do whatever it takes." If your answers are **"Yes"**, then you're ready to go full blast in pursuing your dreams. However, if your answers are **"No"**, then I want you to reevaluate seriously how your purpose and goals align, and why you chose these goals in the first place. Doing this will prevent you from wasting money, time, energy, and relationships. For example, I have seen too many people hustle hard to set up a savings account, pay a credit repair company, and hire a broker to help them get the keys to their new home. But as the pressure begins to build, they get weary and tired of the hassle. The excitement of buying a home is now an investment that taps into and interferes with their current lifestyle. We all know that's a no-no. So midway in the process, they **STOP!** They stop saving. They cancel their repair subscription. And they fire the broker. Goal unaccomplished, but what went wrong? They were off to a great start, but couldn't finish the race. If you go back and look at the investment itself, look at what they lost versus what they would have gained if they had remained committed. Achieving goals are just like this scenario, so commitment is the key to achieving. If you are not ready to commit, that's okay. I would much rather you're honest and happy than miserable and broke.

Affirmation

Feel free to cut these affirmations out and add them to your Vision Board

I enjoy the challenge of a meaningful, worthwhile goal.

I believe in myself!

I easily stay focused on my objectives despite interruptions and distractions.

My goals fit perfectly with all areas of my life.

<u>Keep Your Goals Visual!</u>

Before we get started on the next phase of Activating Your Vision, I want you to think about ways you keep your goals visual and answer the questions below:

Am I successful in achieving my Goals? Why or Why not?

_____

_____

_____

What Visual Tools do I use to remain on track?

_____

_____

_____

Are they working for me?

_____

_____

_____

What am I going to try now to obtain different or better results?

_____

_____

_____

Now that you have our goals listed and know what you need to do to activate your new mission. You need to understand the concept of visual reminders and how they help you remain focused and diligently connected to executing them. The key to activating your goals is to have them somewhere in plain sight, so you'll be consistently reminded of them. Visual stimulation is the best way to keep you on track with your goal. The saying, "Out of Sight, Out of Mind" is what keeps people away from reaching the finish line. This statement comes to life because they lost focus. They lose sight of what matters. We all know that we are pulled in different directions throughout the day. Between work, spouse, children, extra-curricular activities, planning a conference, paying bills, and going grocery shopping. Let's not forget flying to conferences, putting gas in the car, talking to a friend, and trying to find sleep. We often forget to do the task at that we **really** needed to get done.

Let's be honest for a minute; are you guilty of getting up in the morning with a well thought out **to-do list** ready to get the day started. However, you end up going to bed that night realizing you haven't done any of the **to-do** things on your list? *Raising my hand!* I know I am. But why is that? It's because you're all over the place trying to be a great wife, wonderful mother, and an outstanding employee. You forgot to be **productive** for yourself. You forgot about your goals and the things you wanted to accomplish. When it comes to your goals, you have to remember to keep them in the forefront of your mind. It's within your dreams where your true happiness lies. Have you ever heard of the phrase, "Happy Wife, Happy Life"? It's the same thing as, "Activate Dreams, Activate a Better Lifestyle". A lifestyle that provides you nothing but satisfaction, prosperity, and purpose is the place we are all trying to arrive. There are various tasks that can help you reach your ideal lifestyle. I recommend the following:

- **Post-it-notes** ~ Visualizing your day beforehand and reflecting on your time after the fact can set you up for success.

- **Note Cards** ~ Index cards are perfect for capturing ideas on the go, reminding you of what you need to do, and prioritizing them.

- **Vision Boards** ~ Visual posters filled with all of your goals in one place are a perfect way to remain on track with everything you plan to achieve within a specific timeframe.

- **Become a part of your goal** ~ Volunteering or visiting where you wish to be is a visual fantasy for anyone. "Go there, before you get there," helps you see yourself succeeding in the end.

- **Create a Visionary Team** ~ There is nothing like a team or a network of people who can lead, guide, mentor, and promote your dream for you.

Affirmations

I plan my work, and I work my plan.

Each of my goals is assigned a date, and I expect to achieve it.

I have the power to achieve any goal I desire.

I expect the best.

I live a life of
consecutive wins.

Create an Activate Vision Board

Organic Vision

Now, to the best part of your journey; creating your "Vision Board". Not an Ouija Board or some other type of question and answer system for channeling foreign spirits, hoping they can answer organic questions. Only you hold the answers to these questions. Please leave the spook out of this phenomenally creative visualization process. Vision Boards are designed to be enlightening, and inspirational, and a safe place where you can be creative without judgment. There are no set rules for creating your vision board. It only requires an open heart and the power of belief.

Vision Boards are also not created to give you answers; they're created to give you the permission and confidence to understand that **YOU ARE THE ANSWER.** God gave you the answers for free. Vision Boarding is just a tool to help you understand this. I started using Vision Boards while in a hopeless place. They helped me to look at what

I could be, the places I could go, and the things I could accomplish. It gave me a sense of freedom.

"Make the decision to give yourself the gift of your own time as you explore the happiness that is within you. It doesn't cost a thing, and it's full of the greatest riches!" -- Jane Beach

Often we place restrictions on what we believe we can be, do, and have. These restrictions couldn't be farther from the truth. Many of you go through life with restrictions, placing other people's agenda on your time from the moment you wake up to the moment you go to sleep. Some of you aren't even sleeping because you're so busy with other people's claims on your mind. You're living a life of chaos to meet other people's needs and focusing less on fulfilling your purpose. Give yourself permission to STOP the madness. It's not selfish of you to focus on your dreams.

Here are some ways to use your Vision Board for inspiration:

- Help you organize your goals

- Help you focus on taking daily action and completing your to-do list

- Use as a bonding tool with your kids

- Help to ignite your bedroom and boardroom fire

- Help you see what dreams you and your mate share

- Help to focus on your company or personal life vision

- Boost employee morale

- Finish your book project

- Jumpstart your business

Hold up. Wait a minute. Better put some thinkin' in it.

More than Cutting and Pasting!

Here are some things for you to consider before you grab the scissors and glue:

1. Keep Your Head in the Sky and Feet on the Ground

Anything is possible in life. You can and will accomplish great things. Creating a vision board puts your intentions on blast. You get a chance to look at your desires every day. Your Vision Board is the rope of hope you need when your back is against the wall. It's the hope you need when everything seems confusing and complicated. Images make your vision simple. God loves a cheerful giver. What do you think will happen when you become a positive thinker, a productive doer, and a go-getter who keeps your head in the sky and your feet on the ground?

2. Spread Your Wings and Fly

Vision Boarding is about releasing and going back to that five-year-old who was courageous and fearless! As you prepare yourself to attend the Activate Your Vision Board Party or any Vision Board Party, give yourself permission to be excited about the impossible and unimaginable. Thoughts about a lack of money, time, support, or love has no place in the creative visualization process. It would be a disgrace for you to have wings to soar and not even use them because of self-limiting beliefs. Get ready to fly!

3. You have Choices

Keep in mind that you give your life meaning because you have been put here for a purpose. Get rid of any regrets, unforgiveness, or expectations that you have hoarded from others. Think about the power of choice. You are here today because of the decisions you have made yesteryear, whether they were good, bad or indifferent. Make the choice to let go of being perfect, getting it right or knowing what to do. Vision boarding is about being visually active and detached at the same time.

4. There is No Right or Wrong Way to do YOU

Don't allow your thoughts to confuse you. Don't let them tear your heart into pieces. Make the decision to remove the power of the inner critic that dilutes your creativity. Five years ago, I was asked a simple question. It changed my perspective on life. *"What are you pretending not to know?"* Creative visualization is more than just cut and paste; it's making the statement that you're taking out time to stand up for yourself and what you believe.

Your vision board will come to manifestation when you make a solid and persistent connection to your purpose. When your visions are supported by a "why" that has a meaning, you'll find the "how" to bring them to reality.

Three Mistakes to Avoid While Vision Boarding

I'm constantly amazed at the things my son does. He can take some items out of my purse and make a fort. Have you ever noticed what happens when you give a group of toddlers some random items to play with for fun? Things get zesty. They end up drawing or creating something that they're extremely proud of making. They end up putting some pieces together to see what awesomeness they can create or build. Their creative wheels begin to turn, and their imagination just runs wild.

What do you think happens when you give the same bag to some teenagers? Things go from zesty to testy. The teenagers begin to ask questions. What's in the bag? Is it silly, dumb, or childish? They're no longer focused on being creative. Instead, they focus on image and appearance. They either wait to be told what to do, or they refuse to do anything at all.

Now, give the same bag of random items to some adults. They won't have the foggiest idea what to do. They'll begin searching the bag for instructions. They'll look to see what and how it the random items go together. There's no zest and no test. Just where are the instructions, so they can do this the "right way".

You're the adult in this bag scenario. Admit this to yourself, so you can unleash your inner toddler while creating your Vision Board.

To set your creativity on fire, avoid making the following mistakes:

Mistake #1. Thinking that you're making a mistake is a mistake. Don't focus on a perfect layout or the perfect images. I challenge my attendees to make the best board they can with what they have at this moment. I constantly remind them that there are no mistakes and no right way to do it. Just create without rules. Leave the perfectionist and control freak out of it. They don't belong in your creative, safe place.

Mistake #2. Being embarrassed by not reaching previous goals. Let's go back to the scenario of the toddlers with the bag of random items. If what they're creating doesn't work, they find another way, and another way, and another way. Don't be embarrassed by putting weight loss on your board for the umpteenth year. Be honest with yourself and be free. Give your embarrassment a timeout and no dessert after supper.

Mistake #3. Setting no intentions, but expecting results. Creating a Vision Board isn't like waving a magic wand and having the life you want to appear magically. It takes work, a high level of persistence, and tenacity. Let's use the example in **Mistake #2** with the objective of losing weight. The goal is to paste inspirational words and images of living healthy. You may have to cut images of friends smiling, words that speak of loving yourself, and anything that'll support you in living a healthy lifestyle. I encourage you also to be specific on how much weight you want to lose. Looking at salad on your Vision Board every morning may not motivate you. However, looking at a salad next to a picture of a fit body, an attractive person, your favorite vacation spot, and a swimming suit just might trigger some positive energy. The more specific you are, the better. Pick images that'll trigger your emotions into an action. When your visions are supported by a "why" that has meaning, you'll find the "how" to bring them to reality.

Now that you've created your Vision Board lets look at how you can use it every day.

Here are different ways your Vision Board can empower you:

- Look at your Vision Board first thing in the morning

- Look at it throughout the day to feel the inspiration it provides

- Hold it in your hands and internalize the future it represents

- Read your affirmations and inspirational words aloud

- See yourself living in that manner

- Feel yourself in the future, you've designed

- Believe it's already yours

- Acknowledge any goals you've already achieved

- Acknowledge the Law of Attraction

- Look at it before going to bed

Affirmations

Feel free to cut these affirmations out and add them to your Vision Board

I write down the action steps needed to reach my goals.

My written goals are helping me to achieve my life's purpose.

I write my goals down and review them regularly.

<u>Activating Your Goals</u>

When I speak about "Activating," I'm referring to making something active, to apply movement. We can sit and talk all day about our visions, goals, dreams, and thoughts, but they mean nothing at all if you don't apply some movement to them. For example, let's say your dream in life is to become a famous author. You set your goal for it, you put it on your Vision Board, you create affirmations around it, but then you don't write the book. That's the purpose. It's also the reason Activating or putting life into our goals is important. I have yet to see goals, execute themselves or jump off my Vision Board and manifest just the way I need them to. Instead, I had to work hard. I had to educate myself on the mission I want to pursue. I had to become engrossed with the concept of empowering. I had to believe in myself to know I had the gift that could change lives. I had to connect with the right people within the coaching and self-empowerment industry who would give me a platform while I was creating my own. This Activating movement didn't just land in my lap; it took faith, understanding, and the spirit of deserving for me to get where I am. I need you to understand nothing will ever come easily. Sometimes it comes at a cost that many of you can't afford, but in all things know God can support you until your goals become your reality. You'll fall a couple of times along the way because many of your goals will place you in uncomfortable places and unfamiliar surroundings, preventing you from thinking rationally or out of fear. Know it's within that uncomfortable setting where your goals will find the power to grow. But they may grow into something too major for you to handle. That's why you must be knowledgeable and unstoppable in your approach.

Now, I want you to think about how you're activating your goals. What are you doing to make your goals manifest in your life? Think about your movement and list it below.

What am I doing to Activate?

1. _____

_____

_____

2. _____

_____

_____

3. _____

_____

_____

Here are some strategies you can use to help you as you Activate your goals:

- Identify where you are currently, so you can make the necessary changes.

- Set and follow a plan that's efficient and easy to follow.

- Identify and go after your ideal career.

Identifying and being honest with your progress will keep you on track and keep your goals relevant to what it is you're trying to achieve. Another way to keep you activating is by having a close friend or someone you can trust be your accountability buddy. Many have proven that individuals are more likely to achieve their goals when they're held accountable to them by others. Knowing that you have to report your progress to someone else will motivate you to get things done. Accountability is also beneficial for you because your success will be recognized and acknowledged by the other person. Accountability provides positive support! The consistent shoulder to lean on will remind you that you're not alone.

Some people also choose to create accountability by making an announcement of their goals or intentions on social media. By posting your goals, you allow your friends to remind you of what you wrote, motivate you to get it done, and offer their assistance to move your progress along faster. Being held to your word not only creates forward momentum and success, but it also will increase your level of self-trust, self-confidence, and self-esteem.

"On this day, God wants you to know that humans learn only by trial and error, and that includes you. You've got to live life, not think about it. Step into the midst of things, try and fail and learn and stand up again. The question is not whether you will or will not make mistakes - you will. The question *is, do you want to learn and grow, or do you want to shrink back and be stuck? Take that step you›ve been avoiding. You can succeed, or you can get feedback that it didn›t work, but, in either case, you are sure to feel alive.»* ~ *Neale Donald Walsch*

Affirmations

Today, I pay attention to what is most important to me, and I pursue that

Today, I live with purpose and my purpose lights my path to my goals and dreams!

Today, I am taking committed action for my reams. I am on the fast track to them right now

Activate Your Vision in 40 Days

DAY 1 to 10

The POWER OF FOCUS

In today's complex world, you play multiple roles, and you want to excel at everything. You believe "there is never enough time". In essence, the time has nothing to do with accomplishing your vision and everything to do with being present. Focus on the ultimate power that can change the way you think, the way you feel, and what you do at any moment. When you change your focus, you change your perspective on life and all it has to offer. What you focus on determines the direction you'll go. Activating Your Vision comes from mastering your focus. If you fail to focus your energy on the areas that matter you begin to react to things that'll distract you. Some of these types of distractions include:

- **Anything that leads to pain, lack, or frustration**

- **Anything that leads to immediate pleasure and temporary satisfaction**

- **Other people's demands and agendas**

If you want to "Activate Your Vision" in the next 40 days, you must learn to ask better questions. "Activate Your Vision" is a process of taking inspired action that, opens doors. The action will also provide you with a sense of sanity, balance, completion, and leads to the life of flexibility and freedom you deserve.

The first ten days is all about awareness. To maximize the next 40 days, you'll need to remove the unproductive and unnecessary "stuff" that "steals" your time. What activities do you do on a regular basis that you don't have to do, or that you can delegate to someone else to do? What is your current focus? What are some areas you focus on in life that don't serve or support you?

Are there some things you fear experiencing and find yourself thinking about regularly?

Task: Take Out the Personal Trash

We all have unfinished business or unresolved conflicts in our lives.

What we don't realize is how much these things hold us back from Activating Our Vision and living it.

Answer these questions

- Is there a nagging OVERDUE personal issue you haven't handled? This could be a ticket you haven't paid, a tax issue you haven't faced, a bill that's late but you haven't called to speak with anyone. OR anything that is causing you stress because you haven't dealt with it?

- Do you have someone you may have gotten into a fight with but you haven't taken the time to bring resolution?

- Which parent, child, sibling or family member do you need to call and give an apology?

- Who do you need to set free from your mind?

- Who do you have held up because of a past comment, situation or circumstance?

- What part of your body do you need to forgive and treat better? (ouch)

Take out a piece of paper, begin to write down all the little and big things that are and maybe nagging at you on a daily basis personally.

Prioritize the importance of getting them done and start by taking one small action every single day to get this personal TRASH out of your lives.

As you begin to eliminate this stuff from your life, you will feel much more emotionally free. Getting this ground work done will help you push past any obstacles that may present themselves while we are doing the building. My purpose in these assignments is to get you clear and free from any obvious challenges that may arise. We are picking the weeds out right now!

Pick a day that you will be tech free this week?

Pick a day that you will take a verbal fast? (Less talking and more listening). A verbal fast requires a day of you doing more listening and less talking. You will keep away from unnecessary conversations, confrontations, excessive talking. You take this time to listen to EVERYTHING and EVERYBODY.

"When work, commitment, and pleasure all become one, and you reach that deep well where passion lives, nothing is impossible." Nancy Coey

Activation is a mindset, and it is built a little each day, utilizing a vast array of tools. Therefore, please consider adding the positive affirmations written by Catherine Ponder in her best-seller "The Dynamic Laws of Prosperity".

Task: Here are 4 of my personal favorites. I recommend taping them and listening to them every day for the next 15 days until they are fully embodied as an unconscious belief.

"I give thanks that I am now rich, well and happy and that my financial affairs are in divine order. Every day in every way I am growing richer and richer."

"I am now shown new ways of living and new methods of work. No longer am I confined to the ways and methods of the past. I experience my perfect work in the perfect way, which now renders me perfect satisfaction and perfect pay."

"Regardless of taxes, the cost of living or the rate of unemployment, my financial income can and does increase richly now through the direct action of God."

"God's almighty power goes before me, making easy, successful and delightful my way."

DAY 11 to 20

TIMETABLE

Time is a fickle mistress that you either have too much of and will waste on distractions, or you don't have enough time. And you certainly can't control it. More often than not this leads to the gimmes and the wants. If only I had more time I'd:

- **Exercise more**
- **Spend more time with family**
- **Read more**
- **Write my book**
- **Start my business**
- **Clean my Closets**
- **Get out of the house more**
- **Go to that event**

- **Have a baby**

- **Take a nap**

- **Clean my garage**

- **And do more of this**

- **And do more of that**

The Moment of Truth:

I believe there are four categories of time. Some are wasteful. Some are productive. Are you truly productive or is it just an illusion?

Where do you spend your time?

1) Distraction Time: This is when you spend your time on non-important, non-priority task. It's when you just float around and go with the flow with no real direction or inspiration. Shiny objects occupy this space. You often eat when you're not hungry, watch a full TV series, surf the net for hours with no real agenda, or read gossip columns. You're not present in this moment. You're just distracted and looking for temporary stimulation or satisfaction. In my book, *The Road to Redemption*, I call this Mindsturbation.

2) Busy Time: This is when you spend your time on important, but not important tasks. When you feel busy! You're a constant to-do list junkie. One who will spend all of your time creating plans of action, but you get interrupted by the demands of others and get caught up in completing those tasks. You're busy with other people's agendas. You begin to delude yourself into thinking you have to do all of these crazy "to-do" lists that keep you from doing the actions that'll bring you fulfillment. This action means you are just being busy and not being productive.

3) Turbo Time: This consists of handling the urgent and important tasks. Many times these can be unexpected or last minute priorities. These include caring for a loved one, sudden death or birth, and last minute changes or cancelations. These tasks are important and need to be managed by you. Turbo Time requires you to be present, focused, swift in your thinking, swift on your feet, and proactive.

4) Prime Time: This is when you have some important tasks that aren't urgent, but necessary. Many people lose focus during this time because the important tasks should be completed, but you never get to because you "have no time". Not being clear on your priorities and not completing your goals leads to frustration. Prime Time is all about taking care of first things first. Taking action without a true purpose is the drain to a life of fulfillment. People who experience lives of fulfillment spend 60% of their time in Prime Time.

Activating Your Vision requires you to make the decision to find empowering meaning when events in your life happen that are out of your control. There'll be things you cannot control, but you can influence. You must understand you can influence opinions, but you can't control how other people react and their opinions no matter how hard you try. You also cannot control the past - you can't change it. Don't spend your time on what you can't control. For the next 11 to 20 days, work on developing awareness, and eliminating the belief that being busy and overwhelmed is a part of your life. Can you reduce the amount of time you spend in the time zones of Distraction, Busy, and Turbo? You bet your pretty little glitter pen you can! The easiest way to do this is by changing your beliefs about what "urgency" is - URGENT DOES NOT MEAN YOU HAVE TO DO IT NOW!!! You have to stop living in the reaction of outer demands. Start by changing your schedule. When engaged in an activity that you love, time disappears. Make sure you spend your time, energy and focus on what you can control. (This is why Days 11 to 20 are important.)

DAY 11 to 20: DAILY ASSIGNMENT

1) Make a list of things you can't control or influence, but continue to waste time on working.

2) Write down all the reasons why you know those things aren't serious, are ridiculous, and are an insane waste of time.

3) Develop a new belief. Write a simple phrase that you're going to start using as an "incantation" for wasting time. For example, "This is a waste of my time; I'm not going to do it anymore".

To create more time NOW, do the following:

1) Identify activities that aren't important, but because of the sense of urgency you place on them, you spend time doing. Now, do this for things that

aren't urgent OR important, and yet they still waste your time.

2) Estimate how much time you spend each day on these tasks that don't matter or are tasks you could delegate to someone else.

3) Make a list of areas you want to spend time on that would give you a sense of completion and a feeling of being productive and fulfilled. Make the decision

RIGHT NOW to spend a specific number of hours each week on those things that matter most. Repeat after me: I DO HAVE TIME FOR ME!!!!

Goal setting and attainment are best friends. Do something to make sure one of those items on your list happens, and then celebrate.

DAY 21 to 30

THE RESULT

Identify the most important areas in your life that you're going to focus continually on, measure, and improve in both your personal and professional life.

How can you plan your day if you don't have a plan for your life?

There are five main areas of "Activating Your Vision" are Faith, Family, Friends, Finance, and Fitness. Within each of these, there are areas in which you must consistently focus and commit to constantly improve. To determine the areas that you're going to improve, you need to assess where you are right now. Think about your life as if it had five areas you've decided are critically important to improve constantly upon. Think of them as a hand.

The center of your palm presents 0%. The fingers represent 100%. It's hard to get a grip on life, let alone your vision if you can't use your fingers.

Activity

Trace your hand on the blank page below.

(Feel free to cut this out and place it on your Vision Board.)

Each finger represents one of the five main areas. You need to look honestly at your hand and put down a percentage of where you are right now. The object of this is to create more balance in your life, so you're putting your time, energy, and focus on all the areas that matter most to you.

Personal and Professional: (percentage must equal 100%)

Faith: _____%

Family: _____%

Friends: _____%

Finances: _____%

Fitness: _____%

Once you've figured this out and the percentage, write one of the five areas on each finger and post it on your Vision Board.

"Activating Your Vision" comes from a vision that inspires, excites, and drives you. Words can either pick you up or kick you while you're down. Change the language of how you describe yourself by using different vocabulary. These words should be creative and support you in activating. For example, instead of being a School Teacher, you could be a "Purpose Driver".

ASSIGNMENT

Come up with some creative ways to describe your role in your vision. Make your roles playful and fun.

Role Play

Here are some playful and powerful monikers to help get your creative juices flowing:

The Voice of Reason * Fundamentals Expert *
Abundance *Billionaire in the Making *
Protector of the Family Assets * Strategic
Lover * Treasure Hunter * Generous Provider
* Master of Trend Empire Builder * Loving
Daughter * Go to Girl, Nurturer * Force for
Good * Accomplisher * Praiser * Boldness *
Hour of Power * #1 Best-Selling Author Leader
of Leaders * America's Favorite *
#1 Professional Speaker *
#1 Best-Selling International * Creator of Rapport

* Listener * Cheerleader * Dreamweaver *
Success Planner * The "Voice" * Networker
Extraordinaire * Peak Performer * I Can *
Visionary * Doctor of...? *
Teacher Called on by Teachers *

DAY 31 to 40

REWARD

These next few days will be the most intense. Please take your time to play full-out during these 31 to 40 days. Know that, this is where the rubber meets the road. Where the pedal meets the metal. Where the fire meets the wood. I think you get the picture.

Over the course of the next few days, you're going to focus exclusively on writing your vision. If it's not written, it doesn't exist. Have you heard this before?

Day 31: Let's read Proverbs 29:18 "Where there is no vision, the people perish....."

We all need a vision for our lives. A vision gives us purpose, and the drive to move forward. The most successful people all share one thing in common

- they have a clear vision that's so compelling, it creates such passion and enthusiasm. They'll do what the rest of us just merely "talk" about.

Today is the day you must start walking your talk. Having a strong vision will help you through the inevitable obstacles, and detours that come your way when you're trying to attain your goal. Everyone has a vision. Everyone has a purpose. Is your vision driving you closer to your purpose or farther away? How can you tell? Take a look at these key points. Why not go for the big vision? Small visions are just good ideas with no strength to move. Have you ever noticed how people often work harder to make $1000 than they do to make $50,000? Has this happened to you?

If you don't have a big enough "WHY", you'll be wasting your time on a bunch of good ideas that leave you broke and overworked. As you identify your goals, remember your Vision Board doesn't focus on the "HOW". It doesn't contain action steps. You have to activate it. "Activating Your Vision" is the continual process of going beyond your capability and mental capacity to attain your vision. If you don't have a plan for your life, then someone will create a plan for you.

Being an Activator means you're a leader. Leaders create their vision. Leaders also raise their standards from good to great and from excellent to outstanding. To be outstanding, it takes skill and heart.

Here are the best ways to maximize Days 31 to 40:

1) Gather your favorite music - music that'll put you in an empowered, productive, and resourceful state.

2) Get lots of paper and pencils. Or, if you can't write, use a tape recorder. Get plenty of batteries.

3) Pick one goal to work on - then envision yourself having attained the result. How do you look? How do

you feel? How do you act? How do people respond to you? What are your values/beliefs? Make it so real in your mind's eye - make the colors brighter and the sounds crystal clear.

4) Then start writing out this vision in stunning detail, or start the tape recorder and start talking. Take that vision and put it in the time zone of Prime Time!

5) Then write out or tape record your purpose and work your way down.

6) After you create a compelling vision for your life, you want to make sure that it's continually in front of you, to remind you and keep you inspired.

7) Remember, this is an opportunity for you to tap into your creativity! Find pictures of the items you want and place them where you can see them. A

picture truly is worth 1000 words! For example, if you want to lose weight, find pictures of people who have the body shape you want and cut them out! If you want to be debt free, take a big black marker and put paid-in-full or debt-free on your bills. If you desire a specific car or home, take a picture of you standing next to that car or home. It's much more effective if you're in the picture. You're making this so real that your subconscious can't tell if it's real or not, thereby, creating opportunities for you to actualize your vision!

Earl Nightingale said in the Strangest Secret – "You become what you think about." When you review your Vision Board on a consistent basis, and you have a plan for its attainment, you're constantly thinking about it, it'll happen!

Have fun "Activating Your Vision". I sure had fun putting this playbook together for you. Keep in mind Activators are successful people who do things that the failures don't.

Maintain Your Activation

Commitment

Throughout this playbook, I talked about Commitment. I define Commitment as, "doing something in the same manner, way after the emotion that I said it in has gone". I often find that we make quick decisions and commit to achieving something, but move slowly as the excitement falls. Whatever emotion you speak your goals in should be the same emotion you activate in. When you make a hasty decision out of joy, excitement, or eagerness, you make decisions without purpose. Emotional decision-making is the quickest way to fail when it comes to activating your dreams. Your goals can only manifest in a stable and assuring state of mind. When you make a decision using an emotion, you often doubt it or deny it once the realization of the work involved surfaces. For example, have you ever been to a Vision Party or an Empowerment Conference and the speaker is feeding you everything you need to hear? They're breathing life into your spirit, hope into your inner being, and joy into your mindset. You get fired up and ready to execute. You use the affirmations they say to embrace the concepts taught, and network with others to form a buddy system to stay devoted to the lessons learned. Then you go home, sharing your experience with your friends and family while posting it on your social media pages. You can't stop smiling, and you feel inspired to move forward with the life you desire. But as the days go by, you go back to your usual life. Your emotions from the event become replaced with your kid's homework, work deadlines, personal matters, financial stress, and household life.

By the time you look up again, it's six months after the event. It and the emotions you once experienced completely faded until your friend asks you how your activating process is going. Then you remember what you said during the workshops and immediately run to your closet to find that all of the material from the event is still neatly tucked into the bag you had that day. What do you do next? This example shows why emotional decision-making is unhelpful when it comes to committing to something. Now you feel like a failure, and you beat yourself up because you didn't stay focused or committed.

This kind of behavior can have a negative impact on how you approach goal-setting and activating in the future. Not remaining committed to what you promised yourself can make you stop trying to do better and cause you to remain complacent in the life you know you don't deserve. If this has ever happened to you, I am here to comfort you and say, forgetting is common, especially when it's not a part of your current lifestyle. However, for your goals to manifest you must insert them into your life. Making them a part of your day-to-day life will keep them fresh and embedded in your mind and make you think, investigate, strategize, plan, and execute within the timeframe you set forth.

Here is a list of ways you can remain committed to your goals:

5 Key Ways To Remain Activated and Committed

1. **Become Invested in Your Goals** ~ When you invest in your goals, you give 100% of yourself freely, whether it's time, money, sleep or free time. Some part of your goal should be implemented daily regardless if it's learning more about it or networking with others to see how to bring it to fruition.

2. **Free Your Mind** ~ Before you can commit to your goals, you need to remove unnecessary clutter and unfinished business from your life. Your goals need a place to rest, develop, and grow. They can't mature in a mind that's full of past baggage, unfinished goals, and unproductive drama.

3. **Sacrifice** ~ A primary key to knowing you're committed is when you're willing to make sacrifices to achieve your goals. Commitment to sacrifice also relates to the concept of loyalty. Do we stand by your commitment, even though it'll cause interruptions in other areas of life?

4. **Purpose** ~ To have the commitment you must find meaning and purpose behind the mission you're pursuing. Purpose is similar to passion, and the development of a passion that spurs you toward your mission is half of the battle when it comes to achieving goals. Without an inner sense of purpose and motivation, it becomes much more difficult to sustain commitment.

5. **Determination** ~ Determination and commitment go hand-in-hand. There'll be inevitable setbacks along the way to achieving success, and without the determination to overcome these, your commitment begins to waver.

Affirmations

Empowered thoughts and determined action are manifesting my dream faster than ever today!

Today the road to my goals has green lights as far as I can see.

I AM going to DO Better?

Activate Your Vision Recap

- Create Your One-Year and 90-Day Goals, make them heart-centered.

- Understand the difference between a goal and outcome. A GOAL is an idea with a deadline. An OUTCOME is a strategy for how you're going to achieve it!

- What do you want?

- Why do you want it?

- What specific actions do I need to take to achieve this outcome?

- When you know your outcome, you never lose sight of your real target. If you know your purpose, you have the power and passion of finding your way to it. When you have a flexible action plan, you have unlimited choices on how to make it happen.

- CLARITY IS POWER!!!!!

- Write down everything that pop's into your head that you have to do today - ideas, projects, emails, phone calls, etc.

- CREATE YOUR MASTER PLAN. Give each action item a priority by numbering it. ("1" being most important)

- Place an asterisk next to the action items that are a "MUST" for you to accomplish and that'll create the most significant progress toward the completion of your outcome.

Remember, 20% of your actions will give you 80% of your results.

- Establish the duration for each task.

- Estimate the amount of time to complete each action item

- COMMIT YOUR TIME, RESOURCES, AND RESPONSIBILITIES. Number your goals and outcomes based on the priority in which you desire to complete them.

- SCHEDULE those items that have a specific time and can't be moved. Schedule blocks of time to work on other outcomes.

- When planning your day, you have to schedule items that must take place at a specific time first (i.e., Dr. Appointment, school, meetings, etc.) These are times that cannot be changed.

- When you schedule, remember this - no plan will be worthwhile unless you provide the purpose to make it happen - COMMITMENT! Remember, 80% of the battle in achieving a result is finding the emotional drive to follow through. It's imperative that you must train yourself to make it a "MUST" to do whatever it takes to achieve your result. The remaining 20% of the battle in achieving the result is the mechanics - the "HOW", strategy, timing, etc. You must set aside specific blocks of time to work on specific results.

- MANAGE, MASTER, CELEBRATE!!!! Go through your list and check off items that you have completed, not completed. Then, go to your journal section and CELEBRATE! Write down the following:

1) Capture your achievements (i.e., did you achieve a specific result today - worked out, got this assignment done, etc.).

2) Capture your magic moments (i.e., laughing with friends, hugging someone you love, watching a sunset).

3) Create a list of rewards or how you plan to celebrate (i.e., have your favorite lunch or buy a new pair of shoes).

- Start Planning a Project. Think of a project you want to accomplish. Maybe it's something important that you've been putting off because it seems too big (i.e., losing weight, starting a business, planning a wedding, etc.).

Conclusion

Thank you for taking out the time to read on a topic of which I am so passionate. I believe in creating vision boards and journals so strongly that I can't help but spread the message. It's now my life's work. When you begin to write the vision and make it plain, you will understand exactly what I mean. The process has worked for me as well as for many others who have joined me on this life changing journey.

I hope this book has been an inspiration to you.

Gandhi has a wonderful poem I would like to share with you:

Keep your thoughts positive

Because your thoughts become your words.

Keep your words positive

Because your words become your actions.

Keep your actions positive

Because your actions become your values.

Keep your values positive

Because your values become your destiny.

Even though this is the end of the playbook, it's just the beginning of your purposeful Activate journey. A journey filled with goals, vision, and LOVE! I often say, "Activating. It's a lifestyle. Not a game." I believe in this statement because you only get one life to live in this world. To live it to the fullest, you must have a mindset that supports your dreams and desires. My hope is for you to journey into a lifestyle where you're happy, healthy, and successful. Use this playbook as a tool to help you create this necessary mindset. Embrace it and all of your unbridled potential. You have the right to be successful both personally and professionally.

Now go forth and Activate!

About Lucinda Cross:

Lucinda Cross the Chief Activator, Best Selling Author, Speaker, and Spokesperson. Known as the Go-to Girl for Taking Massive Action. Ultimately her work is about helping women live a life of fire, fun and freedom.

Lucinda Cross is a best-selling author, internationally known speaker, spokesperson and energetic teacher of personal and professional development. In 2006, she started the brand Activate Your Life Today! A leadership services firm that specializes in the delivery of personal and professional development enrichment programs. Lucinda creates and delivers products and services that include, but not limited, to seminars, workshops, curricula and training that are developed for professional women, young adults and at-risk women and youth. Her programs are captured to enriching the lives of professional women seeking personal growth.

Lucinda wrote a self- help and empowerment best-selling book, The Road To Redemption (#1 Amazon/ Women Education/ Self Help), which teaches readers the five foundations of living an extraordinary life against all odds. She is also a contributing writer to 4 other best-selling books geared towards leadership, life success strategies, and empowerment.

In her new book, Lucinda continued to empower women along with 23 co-authors, who shared their personal stories to help women win, thrive, prosper, rise in their life journey. The Art of Activation is a life changer and will give you key tactics and strategies to run in hot pursuit towards your personal, professional and global purpose.

Founder of the popular Activate! Conference. Held annually, Activate! Presents a series of informative events with the purpose of "activating" the power inside of women. The conference draws women of every kind, along with leaders from every industry, to discuss topics women want and need. They are encouraged to live fearlessly and effectively.

Lucinda is the personal and professional development expert for several non-profit organizations, business development centers, and her leadership advice have been featured on, The Today Show, AriseTV, SModa- International Spain Magazine

The New York, Fox 5 News NY, News 12 NY, NY 1, The Daily News, The New York Times, Essence Magazine Jan. 2015 Issue, Ebony Magazine, ABC Money Matters, Black Enterprise, Dr. OZ, The Bethenny Show, CNN iReport, Hot97 Street Soldiers with Lisa Evers, Tom Joyner Morning Show, as well as numerous online publications and over 100 online radio shows.

Personal Story

She was only 18, a college freshman, her entire life in front of her; and with one, life-altering choice, it changed.

The campus views and the liberating spirit she had just about grown accustomed to were replaced by the dull images of gray cement floors, painted yellow lines, and the removal of her freedom. Her poor choice, one that she fully accepts as her responsibility, landed her in the federal pen for four-and-a-half years.

Since that time, she had been on fire to inspire, encourage, and uplift women. She teaches them how to learn from their experience, tap into their gifts, and greatness, and build a business that makes a difference to them and to others.

Lucinda Cross-Otiti resides in Westchester NY, with her Husband Bayo Otiti and her three children.

Made in the USA
San Bernardino, CA
22 October 2017